Caught
in the
Moment,

A collection of poetry and prose by
Linda U. Foley

Library of Congress Catalog Card Number
91-090132

ISBN 0-9629147-0-3

Printed in the United States of America

Published by LUF Enterprises.

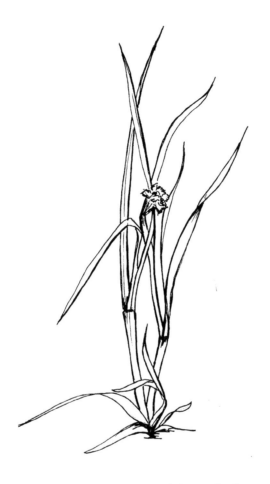

*This book is dedicated to Mike and Christy
that they may perceive and hold special
each and every moment of their lives.*

CONTENTS

This book could not have happened without the support of my family and friends. In appreciation of them and in memory of Alma Ralston, my sincere thanks.

NIGHT QUIET

I whistle in the dark. My sister sleeps next to me, her headboard kitty-corner to mine. My parents' double bed, empty against the far wall. The black-and-white rocking horse stands mutely on my mother's side of the bed, nodding. On Christa's side of the bed, the wardrobe, looking glass glinting in the moonlight.

It is cold. Sometimes there is ice on the walls. A thin sheet of it. The tip of my nose is cold. On the other side of the bedroom door is the kitchen with its wood-burning stove. Not too long ago, I burned myself. The coffee heating in the long-handled pot was scalding and I screamed. Now, I have a scar and I carefully walk past the stove.

We spend much time in the kitchen because it is warmest. From the window, I can see *Frau* Osterman's sunflowers and I can hear the clanging of the gypsies' wagons when they come and hunker down outside the city. When we misbehave, we are threatened that the gypsies will take us. They knock on our front door and ask to sharpen our knives. They are dark and dirty but they wear bright yellows and reds, jingle when they walk. They speak a strange German as if they had just found the words along the way.

Now, everything is quiet. I whistle loudly and tunelessly. I've just recently learned how. My parents always whistle. When she is not singing, my mother whistles bent over her knitting, doing crossword puzzles, sewing, cooking, hiking into the woods, digging up treestumps for firewood, which is against the law. My father whistles when he pulls us around in a little wooden cart, tallies numbers for his reports. He whistles when my mother wears her lavender lace dress. It was her wedding dress once.

I puff up my cheeks, now and then a whistling sound. I am a year older than my sister. I cannot let her know that I am afraid. My cheeks, puffed like balloons, whistle past my night-deafened ears.

Before my parents left, they kissed us and said, "*Schutzengel passt auf*." I really want to believe that my guardian angel is near me. I whistle tunelessly, loudly, into the dark space between the large windows where I think my guardian angel waits with glowing wings high up on the wall.

The train rattles by. I imagine its white plume like dragon's breath trailing in the cold night air. The bells of *Sankt Wunderburg Kirche*. An airplane above. I want to fly. Fly silently like a guardian angel, looking down, watching over other children. My wings glow, swoosh, dip elegantly over the hills, the churches, so many sleepers.

Upstairs, I hear coughing, shuffling, spitting from *Herr* Roessert. I don't think he likes children. He and his sister are the landlords. They both look very much alike. Their skin is grey like potato peels, teeth clacking when they speak, even their clothes are grey and faded like their eyes. The Roesserts go to sleep and rise with the sun.

I whistle. I wish I were old enough to go out, too. Six is too young. Even for bowling. Tomorrow is school. I hate the nuns. They beat everybody with twigs and sticks. Georg's knuckles bled. I felt sick. Sick like when I threw up when they put me onto the large swing during recess. I wanted to cry and run away but I hid behind an enormous chestnut tree. Sister Marta swooped down like an angry crow, black feathers flying, and dragged me to clean up my own mess. Maybe that's why nuns wear black, because they are mean. That's why angels wear beautiful shimmering light things because they are good. God would never wear black. Maybe that's why night is so scary, because it is black. Not a friendly color.

I hear a bicycle bell. Someone heading for his shift at Bosch, to make sparkplugs, at the end of *Geisfelderstrasse*. He is also whistling. Maybe it is not a man. So many women work there, kerchiefs on their heads. Hard work. My mother works in the laundry and it, too, is hard work. I don't like it there, it is so steamy, slick, it is even hard to walk on the wooden planks. Something always hisses and drips. I don't like to walk over the wide cracks between the wooden planks. Like walking over a wooden bridge - it makes my stomach tingle. I can't look down. Something tries to pull me downward. I feel sad when I see my mother scrubbing on the large tables with the linens and shirts slathered, looking like flat, wet noodles. Her pretty face turns red, her blond hair hangs limply and I can't hear anything she says. Scratch, scratch! The noise of the bristles on the wet fabric makes my hair stand up.

I like quiet places. Not night-quiet. It is so still, my ears hurt from listening so hard. The room feels heavy. I wait, counting the dark minutes, waiting for the key to turn in the front door. I wait for my parents to tiptoe in, to bend in the glow of the wall-light into my bed to kiss me. They will say, "Aren't they good, *unsere Kinder!* Aren't they beautiful?" not knowing that I am awake under my closed lids.

But, until I hear their quick footsteps, their murmurings and laughter along the pavement, until I hear their key in the front door, I'll keep on whistling, looking at that dark, mysterious space between the windows...

PAPER ANGEL

My favorite teacher is standing at my extreme right. *Fraeulein* Rothenberger is a part-time teacher. She's tall and gangly and a wonderful artist. Hers is the drawing on the upper portion of the blackboard. Mine is the winter scene on the bottom. I know Annie Hornauer must have said something nasty when she saw my drawing as she came into class this morning. She always wants to be better than me.

I feel silly holding this paper angel. I am ten years old, perhaps old for my age. My mother always says, "You're missing your entire childhood."

My green knit sweater is pulling under my arms and across my chest. The waist on my dress is getting high. I am developing. The photographer is still fidgeting with his camera. As he gets ready to hold the flash up high, I lower my arm somewhat and hold the angel in front of my chest.

On my left is *Fraeulein* Kratzer, our full-time teacher. She loves the girls who come from professional homes. My father is a chauffeur for *Herr* Seiffert, an importer of cotton. I remember the first day I came into this class. I was already nervous and somewhat late which meant that forty pairs of eyes stared at me while I stood in the doorway. I was given a desk to share with Margot Pechmann. During the penmanship lesson I neglected to skip the top line of the page and when *Fraeulein* Kratzer walked along the aisles, she saw my mistake. Without hesitation, she reached across Margot and slapped me a stinging blow.

I smell the candles to my left. Soon, the heat rising from them will be turning the wooden propeller on top of the candle stand. Christmas tree branches are decorating the room. It smells cozy. The late afternoon light has settled on the window sill and snow encrusted on the window frame glitters blue.

Marianne Kettman is holding the lantern she had made for *Sankt* Martin's Day. Sometimes I don't like her even though she's always been very nice to me. I have been to her house several times but I never feel quite right there. Her mother is always home while mine works. Marianne's father is a graphic artist and works behind a large desk in his home. He works for many of the German film producers.

Margot Pechmann is on the other side of the blackboard, hunkered down like everybody else waiting for the photographer to give us the signal to smile. She has become my best friend. Her mother also works. *Herr* Pechmann was killed in the war.

Even though I am not looking, I know Maria behind me is practicing her glamor smile. This week she has wanted to be an actress. Before that, she wanted to be a nun. Her family owns the cinema across the street. During the summer she had invited me one afternoon. We went into the garden, drank lemonade. She collected jagged pieces of glass and heaped them on one sunny spot. She invited me to kneel down upon them with her, initiating proper suffering, to test herself as a future nun. I wonder what she will want to be after Christmas.

Baerbel Zenkel stands in the front row, smiling broadly. Her desk is right in front of mine. Everybody picks on her because she acts so uppity, speaking her high-German. I think her face looks handpainted like some of the *Kaethe Kruse* dolls. Just two weeks ago, she had her braids cut. They were beautiful, auburn and thick, unlike mine which are thin and ratty. The others would yank on her hair, call her names, make fun of her diction. Anyway, this week, Baerbel thinks she is too good for me.

The photographer holds up the silver pan and a white flash follows.

OMA

I remember
my grandmother's soapy smell
soft skirts   deep wrinkles of
her hands shelling peas
braiding my hair and
together we braced

elbows on window sill
as she whistled softly   waiting
for evening to settle
in marketplace
below
bronze fish spouted

We hung grandfather's twilled trousers
and handkerchiefs stained from snuff
high above red-tiled roofs
When Vesper bells tolled
Danube shores glowed pink
we prayed together

Her breath nudged me into sleep

JOURNAL

Bamberg, den 24. Januar 1958

We have said good bye everywhere. Our rooms are empty. White spaces from pictures are on the walls. Cupboards are empty. Some glass wool in the hallway; the packers have been here for a week. We carried washbaskets of dishes, clothes, books, downstairs to the big crates in the yard. Everything is gone and waiting somewhere for us in a hazy place called America. From here on, our lives will be different.

It is our last night here. We are sitting with the relatives. My father is arguing with his older sister, Trina, about the Russians, a better future, America! The family is quick-tempered. My father sets his beer bottle down sharply. His eyes flash.

I see Christa, my sister, across the table from me swallowing hard. She pushes her blood sausage around on her plate. No one wants to know what we think. We are only 13 and 12 years old. Since I am the older, I can't let my sister see how terrible I feel.

The heated words rush past my ears like an angry river. Of the family, no one has ever left. A ship called 'Ryndam' will take us from Rotterdam, Holland, to New York.

America, February 1958

My sister and I are the new girls in this school on Long Island. I think we are the only Germans here. Hundreds of students flow along the hallway, patrolled by other students wearing armbands for identification.

So many new things. A bright redhaired girl to my right wears her sweater turned around. She has an unusual name - Joan. I have trouble with the J sound. I can hear myself saying Tschoan. Everyone laughs. I try to avoid calling her anything.

After class has ended, Jimmy and John are waiting for me. (Tschimmi and Tschon). They want to carry my books. Why? I am capable. They laugh.

Denise comes rushing at me. I feel ugly. She is Snow White with long slender legs, jet black hair to her shoulders, deep blue eyes, bright red mouth. I quickly lick my lips to give them shine. She has clusters of sugar cubes hanging all over the front of her blouse and on her hips. I don't understand. What does 16 have to do with sugar? She asks me when my birthday is. I am very confused.

~~~

I am sitting at Henry's desk in a small room called a den. Henry and his wife, Gina, were our best friends in Germany. Christa and I were flowergirls in their wedding. When they left Germany six years ago, they had promised to send us 'papers.' They are our sponsors.

~~~

We have been in America six weeks. Every day is different. But every morning, I think I will walk into the sunshine of my old world, with my old friends and a world I understand. I know now, that my life will never be the way it was. I am going to be someone else...

~~~

I hear Christa talking with Joanne Maggio who lives on the other side of the gas station on the corner. She is short, plump, has a long pony tail, pimples and no chin. She also has a pretty smile and a strict Italian father who will not let her wear make-up. Their house is very plain. They eat sandwiches in front of the television. Mr. Maggio has a crew cut and wears blue coveralls. Mrs. Maggio always wears an apron. Joanne is their only child.

~~~

The Maggio family will take Christa and me to church - a drive-in church.

As soon as we open the wire gate at the Maggio house, the front door opens. Mr. Maggio speaks English with an Italian accent. I understand him less than other people. We smile and nod many times and he pats me on the shoulder and nods some more. Mrs. Maggio smiles, does not speak, but stands behind her husband. I think they are glad that we are also foreign. There are three very small pictures of a madonna and of Venice on the living room wall. There is a large television in the corner, two armchairs, a sofa, two snacktables and a round brown carpet with fringes. It is clean but bare and cold.

~~~

We always shop Friday night. The supermarket has so much of everything and everything is canned, bottled or wrapped. There is so much fruit. We had one peach tree in our garden in Germany and my grandmother guarded it carefully. I am not sure why. There were plum trees in *Frau* Schnitzer's garden next-door. When we played ball, we would "acccidentally" drop the ball across the fence. On the way back, we stuffed our pockets with plums.

The milk is so good here, it tastes like cream. It comes in cartons and in bottles. At home, we had an aluminum container which we took to the milkstore down the street. The milkman would fill it according to request - 1 liter or two liters. On special occasions, we were sent with a light blue glass bowl to have it filled with fresh whipped cream. On the way home, I "accidentally" licked too much of it and then tried to rearrange the cream artfully so the bowl looked full again.

Then, there is ice. Everything is iced or ice-cold. Americans love cold drinks and warm rooms. Just another thing to get used to. Like driving everywhere. Drive to shop, drive to church, drive to visit. It is also strange to bring food home in paper sacks. I miss the butcher shop next door and the bakery across the street which made famous "Hoernla," a flaky croissant. The grocer downstairs gave children lemon or raspberry bonbons if they were polite and patient customers. My old world was so much smaller.

~~~

The bus stop is right outside Henry and Gina's frontdoor. There is a group of students. They are in eighth or ninth grade except for Lenny, who looks uncomfortable carrying a book. His hair curls into the collar of his leather jacket. He smokes.

Johnny has long, dirty blonde hair which hangs in a big loop over his forehead. I think everyone wants to look like Elvis Presley or at the least they all want to look like each other.

Rosalie has pitch-black hair which she wears piled and puffed up high. She generally forgets to comb the back of it. Her lips are crimson. I think she could be pretty if she did not look so artificial. She usually has a wad of gum in one cheek and always talks about Noxema. She has bright red painted nails, mostly chipped. Her skirts are poorly hand-sewn down one side, making them extremely tight. I see the stitches yawning widely. She wears thick white socks and black shoes called loafers. When I stand next to her, I feel too tall and plain. The boys like her.

Danny is skinny like a winter squirrel and always looks cold. His hair is straight, hanging down over his eyes. He tilts his head backwards to clear his eyes which are very pale.

~~~

I am lying on my bed. Christa and I have bunkbeds. Mine is the upper bunk, like a bird's nest. From here, I can see out of the window which is somewhat small and high in the wall. Not a window which you open to lean on the sill to talk to your neighbors and friends. I can hear the clanging of the gas station bell. Cars swoosh in and out through puddles of slush.

I hear my parents murmuring, laughing, in the next room. When I lift my head out of the pillows, I can hear every word. The walls are thin. My mother talks in a kind of singsong like the Spanish women from the sweatshop where she works. She has picked up their rhythm. The gas station bell clangs loud and harsh into our room. The cars pull in, pull out, lights rush in, lights rush out of our room. Tires spin through melted, grey snow. The dog howls.

~~~

The snow is so high. I never imagined that it snowed like this in America. My sister and I have shovelled for over an hour to clear Henry's driveway. The blisters are popping right under my gloves. The snow makes me feel real and I sink into the memory of snow at home. Sledding. Apples on the back of the stove, aroma heady like mulled cider. Churchbells rising on the ebbing, chill wind. New rabbit tracks on untouched snow in the waning daylight. Black barren branches draw sharp blue shadows on molten snow. I watch my breath, feel it flap around my face, reach for my hair. Frozen tendrils at the edges of my eyes.

The sun tries to break through the bleak day. The sky looks grey like spilt milk. The house next door is pink, but in the grey light, looks dirty. I shovel harder. I work away my unhappy feelings.

~~~

There is a "party" next Saturday night. Ritchie who lives on the corner wants to take me there. My parents are concerned. Gina laughs and says, "Reser," (my father's nickname) "all the American kids go to parties. We know Ritchie and his family. They can be trusted." We trust Gina and Henry because they have lived here six years longer and understand the American ways. But, when Gina bought me a lipstick my father looked up sharply and said, "What is that? Throw it out!" Gina said, "Reser, don't be silly, you are in America, you have to learn to act like an American." My father said, "Don't care if we live in China. No!"

~~~

Ritchie will pick me up at eight. The "party" is tonight. I feel very grown. I am wearing a black dress with delicate embroidery along the scoop neckline. It is fitted in the waist with a narrow belt. The skirt falls below my knees. Gina gave me this dress. I am wearing nylons and black slipper-like shoes with little straps. I feel the way I think Americans look - confident.

~~~

There are many boys and girls at the party. No parents. A record player is in the corner. Coca Cola bottles everywhere. Potato chips. Someone is smoking. Someone sings "Beebopalulu..." I don't understand. The lights are very low. Girls and boys are hanging onto each other moving slowly over the square linoleum tiles. I see myself looking stiff and uncomfortable in the large, gold-edged mirror which hangs slightly crooked over the plastic-covered sofa. All the girls are wearing tight skirts, scarves tied at the back of the neck, sweaters worn backwards, or wide skirts of a funny kind of material called felt. I feel old, out of place. I don't know how to dance to this music either. "Marenge." Something to eat? A girl named Fran grabs me and insists on teaching me how to sway my hips from side to side and to drag one leg after the other. Her boyfriend is Joe, who is Spanish.

~~~

Joe is having a party. He lives in a different part of town. I am wearing a grey wool skirt and soft, blue sweater. A blue chiffon scarf tied at my neck trails down between my shoulder blades. Joe is dancing the Marenge with me. Someone turned out the lights. There are no adults. I don't like this but, I don't know what to do about it. Joe talks Spanish with his friends. "*Arriba, arriba...*" He murmurs into my neck. His hands move up until they rest near my bra strap. I feel uncomfortable and don't know what to say. Am I being tested? I can't wait until my father comes to pick me up. Joe walks me outside, insists on kissing me. We are caught in the glare of my father's car lights. I feel terrible on the way home. My father doesn't say much. Looks puzzled. I feel as though something's been lost...

SEPARATE

It didn't matter just where she was
in the hotel   arcade   the mall
or at the beach
        she felt dwarfed

forgot what her face
looked like   she strained to find
        an image of herself   somewhere
a reflection in the water   a window
in sunglasses   or simply people's eyes

Other bodies used up her space
took away her breath
        grabbed at her shadow
Her personal belongings were
        taken up by other people
as if rightfully theirs.

THROBBING SUNLIGHT

The three o'clock schoolbell released me into the light of the spring sun. Again, I am the new girl in school and isolated from the others who walk in fluttering, gossiping groups. Pretending absorption in my new surroundings, I walk alone.

The spring sun, color of a sliced apple. Shadows from the elms along the street spatter on the sidewalk, peeling doorways, sullen gas pump. The red-haired attendant is whistling through his freckles. Sun touches my neck, bare legs, pushes me along, a warm stream. The eastern breeze off the ocean is tangy, settles on my tongue and still-white arms.

The air hums. Sunlight tastes like honey. Laziness, insects, expectations. Like a fat, satisfied cat, the street stretches toward the doorsteps. I, too, feel fat and lazy inside and forget that I am lonely.

On my left, the boarded-up laundromat, then the empty and overgrown lot, a small stretch of wire fencing part of which hangs mid-air. Gerard's Drugstore. Here, the small door to the shop where my mother works. I say I like to surprise her, but I am really looking for reassurance, a warm spot. The door's shellac is cracked, resists my touch. There is one high stair and a miniscule entry. I climb a narrow flight of steps. Thick funnels of dust dance above me. Deep droning bounces off the staircase walls. The noise deepens near the top and the floor vibrates. Dust climbs into my nostrils.

Inside the large room, dark heads bob up, some women wave, others call hello accented in Spanish. My mother is the only blonde head bent intently over a piece of material. Guided by her nimble fingers, it runs quickly under the pecking needle of the machine. Hers is one of nearly a hundred squatty machines whose noise fills the cavernous room, ominous like a disturbed beehive.

Every stitch counts here. This is piece work. My mother is quick, reliable. She does not realize I am here until I am right by her side.

I put my hand on her back, bend to kiss her cheek. Even though she can't hear me above the din, I say, "*Gruess Gott, Mutti.*" She is glad to see me, even though she is rushed. Her lips move in answer to my greeting, "*Gruess Gott, Spatz.*" A gray film of dust sits on her hair, her clothes..

To her left, a large canvas receptacle which holds finished pieces. Mounds of finished pieces. This day my mother had been working on zippers and sleeves. Since she has started to work here, clothing in the department stores has taken on a different meaning for me.

Different women come by, swinging hefty hips. I imagine I see baskets balancing on their heads filled with grapes and bread loaves. Some women catch my mother's eye, gesture in the air with swinging arms, roll eyes at me, yellow-flecked brown marbles. Although everybody yells in order to override the steady noise of the machines, I still cannot make out what is being said. I suspect lip reading. Though I have only been here a few moments, my head is pounding. I am too clean.

Turning from one of the women my mother looks at me, smiles, nods her head and looks back at the woman. Conspirators, women-mothers conspiring in my favor.

My mother rises and pushes the canvas receptacle toward another area where the pieces will be connected to other pieces and shortly, there will be many other dresses to join the waiting legions on the racks. Someone pushes a broom along the wooden floor. Her sweat and raspy voice reach me at the same time. She says something about my terrific Mamma and "Shee's a nica lady." I agree, embarrassed because everything is so simple. We smile fat toothy smiles at each other. I know my mother helps many of these women with their English and I find it amusing. *Mutti* is the only true foreigner here while all the others are native foreigners. Born here, raised in their own particular ghetto. Still, their accents are every bit as real as my mother's and mine. Perhaps some people never yearn to reach out beyond their prescribed and accepted limitations.

I am offered something to drink. An offering to the new, the American generation. I smile but feel angry and inadequate. These women shuffle about with apologetic smiles as if their experiences were inconsequential.

I have not labored and should be the water bearer instead I accept the drink graciously; I am well brought-up. My mother and these women are beating the rocks. I wish to take them to another, a softer place. The woman who gave me the drink smiles as if I had given her a gift.

My head throbs from the steady vibrating noise, my eyes smart from the dust, sweat runs down my sides from the thick heat. Is this the price of liberty, of freedom?

I motion to leave. Someone says, "What a nica girl, so smart... like her Mamma..." I hear my mother's fragmented response, "daughter ...real American..."

The thundering noise of the machines hounds me down the stairs like a gathering storm. The door closes on the dust. I imagine becoming a citizen, a real American, but all I can think about are heavy, sweaty women guiding pieces of material in the heat of a droning, sweltering room. All I see is dust; all I feel is heavy, throbbing sunlight.

PERSPECTIVES

like a tiny grey mole
inside a huge sterile helmet
she curls in the corner of her house
       Watching

as a wide grey blanket
floats toward her window
billows closer
spreads dull moist shadows
across her yard
       She hurries

to draw all curtains
and to stuff all cracks   but
still she feels its
persistence thud darkly
at the glass

damp sheeting nudges
the door along its track
seeps like milk
through the walls
       And she knows

in time   it will bank inside
like frozen snow

OFF RIVERSIDE DRIVE

Though I dream of beech tree trunks, color of seal skin, reality - rooming here with Elisabet off Riverside Drive - is different. Reality is linoleum curling like stale bread. Is the lopsided wardrobe on the far side of the living-room, doors wallpapered with "Fly Lufthansa" posters. Is a curtain-draped window looking into an airshaft. Is a small brown plastic radio from which issues Long John Nebel's voice, Manhattan's disc jockey.

In this smoldering apartment, three flights up - no elevator - I am lonely, the pain, a worm eating my insides. At nineteen, I feel hollow, hungry, isolated.

Elisabet is at work when I am at home. She has two jobs, does not speak English. I, too, am foreign but my English is good enough for the bi-lingual job at Rockefeller Center. Though ten years younger, I feel ten years older than my friend. She relies on me to translate, to explain. I want to lean on someone.

At night, taking my yellow laundry-basket to the vibrating blue neonlights of the corner laundromat, the shadows whisper loudly, insinuate. My head high, nails glinting, no one would think me afraid, would they?

Later, curving upward inside the echoing stairwell, my own shadow stalks me to our green door. The toilet at the end of the hall gurgles. While I fumble with the keys, laundry-basket sitting high on one hip, floorboards creak across the hall. I feel the movement under my feet as I feel the microscopic eyes on the back of my neck through the peepholes. I imagine tiny people clinging to glass eyes, creeping through keyholes, tiny voices calling.

I wonder if it is my youth or my foreignness which isolates me or is it simply an attitude inhaled along with the steam rising from manhole covers, acquired with the paper bought from quick, impersonal hands at the corner? Does the unseeingness that glides over people here like sheets of ice embalm within fear, distrust and loneliness?

I fling open the door which bangs sharply against the wall. In the same motion, I flick on the ceiling light, grab the can of Raid and blow away the dancing black cockroach in the white enameled sink. No matter how we clean and scrub, they are always here, even tottering along the edge of the pantry shelves.

I've lived here just a few weeks, but I am learning to steel myself against these sights, to control my revulsion.

On dismal rainy days, I sit on the black-and-white checkered sofa, huddled in the corner of this crooked house, engulfed by walls which are closing in, my limbs growing into trees, my head a pinpoint. I turn off the light to soften the contours of a reality which overwhelms me. The darkness is not total, it is layers of grey and brown. Squares of light from the window are sharply defined at my feet. The window itself, outlined starkly. A cut-out in a shadow box. I want to be on the other side of it. I feel so locked in. I feel so locked out. The city reflects in the panes. Drops of light shiver in the corner like autumn leaves eddying at the river shore.

Something dark, oval, tiny-legged. A black cough drop moves into a square of light. Bugs. Sometimes they don't even wait until you leave, but are brazen enough to come right out, demand your grilled cheese sandwich with you in full view. I don't want to lower my feet. Some huge and hairy roach hand will reach from under the sofa, grab my ankle and drag me under there. Sometimes I feel the sides of the building buckling under the demands of its scuttling inhabitants. They are drilling the sheetrock like Swiss cheese, drilling each other into finely-tuned soldiers ready to attack in force.

I know my imagination is agitated, but I am caught within myself. I have nowhere else to go, nothing to do except listen to Long John Nebel and I wonder who he really is.

His voice is close, intimate, in my throbbing room. Does his talking merely cover up a small hairy man in a windowless office? Does he have a ghost writer? Does he know where his words fall, that I am here?

I listen to a seance on the radio, the moaning and gibberish do not elevate my mood. I open a window, lean on the gritty sill. A funnel of wind slaps me full in the face. The movement is welcome, preferable to the stillness pounding inside my room.

Honking, calling, slamming doors, clatterings and quick heels rise upward. I could sit quite naked up here on this sill and no one would be the wiser. If I ranted, spouted outlandish things, no one would respond. Thick indifference bumps against me everywhere, threatens to throttle me like the stifling heat hovering in the street.

I want to poke holes, release the laughter, feelings and colors. There must be other shadings of degree than screaming headlines and cabbie-conversations, people hustling in sepia doorways, bag ladies squatting in the folds of voluminous coats and skirts and hugging their bulging shopping bags.

A shadow jumps for the lower rungs of the fire escape below. Clatter. Another kicks a garbage can lolling into the street. Unseen people yell, unseen people walk, unseen people write graffiti.

From the subway windows, beneath crooked elbows, dangling newspapers, graffiti pounds past the windows, some of it red, screaming to be heard. Outrage vented, artwork displayed, recognition sought. My graffiti burns in my head, my gut. I wish I could get it out. Instead, that worm bores away like a red hot drill.

From the river comes the sultry smell of decay, heat, summer. I wait for Elisabet, or morning, whichever comes first. Perhaps morning never comes because there never is a night. The city just slows down into a rumble of simmering grayness, pale left-over night. The river smells fishy, oily, but with the morning light, its odors recede, overpowered by the increasing throbbing, eddying business of the city people.

Morning steals across my sill, grabs me, drags me through the green door, down the groaning steps. Day wraps around me. A white-gray blanket of smog rises and later will lower itself like a settling silent explosion. The heat will wash down my body, drag hair and skin and clothing downward but now... in the new morning light, there is a silver glitter in the sunshine, smell of something blue in the air. I feel white sand dusting my feet, hear screaming gulls, see them swooping into wide blue spaces, see tree trunks, color of seal skin.

Steam rises from the manhole cover. A small dry hand shoots out the morning edition from the corner stand. No one sees behind my city eyes. I've pulled that thin sheeting of ice around me, embalmed, secure, alone.

SEASONS COME AND GO

O ur young family had just moved into our first home. Aflutter with decorating ideas and motherhood, I thought how nice this neighborhood was. How quaint, quiet, almost European. Then, one day, while measuring the windows for drapery material, I saw her. I watched her pass. Her appearance see-sawing past my window added another dimension to my suburban life.

Walking slightly stooped, cracked hands firmly clasped behind her back, she walked past our house many times. Resolutely, she placed one old foot in front of the other as if she had a place to go.

Standing behind the sheer curtains of the nursery, I waited for her to pass the house each day. With her head bent, she walked stopping now and again to admire a tulip or to pat the fuzzy head of a stray dog or cat - lonely strays acknowledging each other.

That was in the summer. In the winter, she walked slowly almost methodically up and down the street as if in search of something. She was always alone. She wore a large coat with her collar turned up to protect her ears from the sharp wind. Sometimes, she faltered slightly on a patch of ice.

In the winter's desolation, her figure cut a stark silhouette and sometimes I wished not to see her. I could feel the wind in her bones. Following an old tattered pattern, her lone figure carried sorrow. She made me fear the future.

I wanted to rush out to stop her, to force time to stand still. When I finally resolved to put my feelings into action, she had moved on. One foot in front of the other, biding time, following an age-old tattered pattern.

THEIR ROOMS

So cool and shadowy
smelling of hamsters
vigor intolerable youth
their sweetness innocent growing
and already victories and defeats

As I reach through their
dirt-caked cleats   music sheets
leotards graded papers
loving notes to me   grubby hugs
and soapy smiles

There like a shadow
slides the thought
behind my eyes
that my ego was justfied

ONE MORE DANCE...

My mirror-image son and I
twirl swirl through the kitchen

      "Another dance tonight"

the girls already like to slip
behind his eyes

      "Put it right there, Sweetheart"

and Bogart smiles again
through 13 years of living

chubby cheeks rumpled hair
fist of worms and red trucks vie
for the proper image behind my eyes

I hold his warmth and new gyrations
on my floor in need of washing

last night still he cried warm brown hair nuzzled
my shoulder I tried to set his world upright

somehow grateful selfish for his tears
collecting words of love each smile and touch

for the time when I will wonder
whether we had danced enough...

THE DANCER

like a gazelle

      graceful   smooth

like the bough of a spring birch

      acquiver

my dancing child

      player of the instrument of

her body unmarred as yet

long muscles tendons and mind

      straining

determined to play

      that graceful tune.

LAST NIGHT

I crept close to her when
I thought she was fast asleep
to hold and test her fingers
warmth vulnerability
her growing

I wanted to squeeze
her softness into a tiny ball
of everlasting memory
into something solid to keep in my palm
something even she can't take away

In the morning I kissed her awake
and marvelled
at her tender
small features growing
under my watchful eyes

Her miraculous greening.

MENDOCINO

Seaslick under his ski-vest, the scuba diver leans against his Landrover. Beer and laughter pass between him and two stout women. Modern *Bruenhildas*, they've come to see what *Siegfried* brought back from the hunt.

Tapedeck music pierces the muggy, thick air. Feeble sunlight strains through the mist, bluish-white like mother's milk. On the other side of the gulch, beyond a strip of gray grass, a small colorful sweater-huddle. Squirming, giggling youngsters from the Caspar Beach Campground across the highway are building a fire. Pale orange smoke wriggles free. Hair whips in the gusting wind, leaping and whirling like floating algae.

Beneath my bare feet, I feel the sand shifting and gritty waves sucking in on themselves. Water laps at my toes rinsing away my footprints. The sea, the elements, swirl around me. Ashy layers of sand and light lift, shift, drift and bank. Light, sand, the afternoon and time itself, rush like shadows through my fingers.

The sea gushes in, hungry-mouthed, nipping the shore, digging beneath the beach, constantly changing the face of the coastline. Rubbing, sanding, polishing driftwood. Waiting.

Above, the gulls are cresting the sky and because the sea's rising mists have obliterated the horizon, they may be flying into the water instead. The birds vanish. Maybe we are all upside down to be swallowed by the gray ghost of the sea.

Other divers dangle like black, slippery eels from the lowered reardoor of the Landrover. Tanks scrape and bump loudly against each other, scratching the muted atmosphere. All sound, coated by the mist, disintegrates into a white thickness like words spoken from a feverish-thick tongue. Yellow and red life-savers, sea anemones, wrap themselves around the men's necks.

Long after we have re-entered the flow of the highway, the sea's thudding, grey heartbeat pounds still in my ears. My veins are filling up. I taste grey, green, salty spittle on my tongue. Foam gushes through me, collects behind my sea green eyes.

MATTER OF TIME

grass is soft and yielding
like memories of other summers

like then
I hear the neighbor's sprinklers
see a fat cat curled in a pool of light
grass fragrant cool cut widebladed
between my dusty toes

I feel a vital part of early evening
as lightning bugs spark
in the deepest part of the willow trees
telephones ring   doors slam
the neighbor's brown house beyond the hedge
glows brilliantly briefly in the setting sun
the white fence draws sharp blue lines
on the discolored patio

like then
my hands sink into the cuttings of
the musky odor of the moment

CAUGHT IN THE MOMENT

Grayness is creeping over the Oakland Hills, getting lighter, beiger, pushing a sogginess ahead of itself. I had hoped for a thunderstorm. If not a storm, at least a drizzle which makes me think of the East Coast, the old house, its cozy, woodsy smell of small rooms...

...outside, dripping leaves and squooshy grass, gutters stoppered up and the cat does not want to go outside, gets her tail caught in the porch door.

Springs of the vinyl sofa squeak on the porch and the air looks brown through the screens. Voices next door seem closer, sultry. Coffee brews in the kitchen, something aromatic is baking. Telephone rings, a friend.

Curtains hang limply on all the white-painted windows, here and there a tired bubble in a screen. The clothesline is astride with drops, their cumulative weight pulls it deep. The gate creaks, wood expanded by humidity. Sparrows and bluejays are washing, blustering, fighting in the puddles on the strangely discolored patio.

I look deeply into the closet, underneath odd-hanging fringes of clothing for an errant shoe. A beige softness strokes my bare shoulder, a forgotten scent rises from flowered folds. At the far end of the deep darkness, the window overlooks the gable of the house, a light at the end of the tunnel. I feel warm, soft and protected in the womb of the house. I think nothing can ever change because I am here, caught up in the very moment because I can see, touch and hold but, already I know that some time, years later, I will be writing down these lines and woe creeps into my stomach. It is already happening. I can't stop it! So, I hold the images, lock them into my mind, hold them with my fingers, hold my own face because I know that it too is slipping from me - it is not mine, like time, only borrowed.

I want to rush down and hold my mother's whistling, my father's warm voice in response. I want to lock their time, my time, together...but, as I am listening, the moment is already passing...

...there's not even to be a drizzle. Outside, it is brightening and the top of the evergreen hedges by my window are streaked with yellow light which is widening, deepening, hanging down the sides like a lace cloth. Christy's beach towel is still draped over the patio chair to dry since yesterday. Now, it is hanging heavy and uninspired but in the gathering light begins to look like a sail, hopeful after the luff. Shadows of the lemon tree leaves are appearing on the wooden planks of the deck. Shadows, an exercise in contrast between light and dark can only happen in conjunction with light. Without light, shadows cannot exist... without the fleeting moments, there is no time at all.

SILENT CHANGES

The sun has burnt white through the fog, leaving the sky licked clean like a china plate.

The door slams. Mike calls, "Love you, Mom, have a nice day." Just yesterday we sat on the sofa and I taught him how to tie his shoes properly.

Al has taken his coffee cup outdoors. I see only the upper part of him. Grey pinstripe, moving along behind the light green growth of the hedge. As in a Punch-and-Judy show, the scenery is propped beyond his graying blonde head - browning hills, rose-bright azaleas.

I watch from my oak kitchen seat, from inside my place of light blue pajamas. Strange seesaw this. This silent movement, growing, separating, leaving such shadows.

I take my cup ("World's Greatest Lover"), nudge the screen door along its track with my elbow. It whispers, glides. I enter unabashed sunlight. White, pale new sun. I feel the anxiety of growth right through the soles of my bare feet, the straining and strengthening of roots, lively juices. The earth has put its mark on me, demanding returns in spades. I feel dry. A chill pure and white radiates from the sky, encircles me in a light of ice.

The wood of the deck has already begun to garner the sun's warmth, which eludes me. I walk down the steps to the lower deck, shake the inner chill, look for confirmation of the immediate moment, hoping that it will last forever, which it won't. Still, I demand the illusion. There, below the steps, I catch for myself the corner of his smile, touch of light eyes, temporary satisfactions like giddy soap bubbles - but worth the wait.

Like a colorless apple blossom, the sun sits in the eastern sky. I feel it blooming huge. Even though I don't see it wandering and changing, I know it is.

Silent play of light on my bare arms, the hairs turned silver in the sunlight. I feel freckles growing. I won't see them until tomorrow. Just because I don't see them does not mean they won't be there. Because Mike ties his shoes properly now does not deny the moment when I taught him how.

In the corner of the deck sits the wine barrel, large and musky. Bright glistening trails from the night's snails upon it. We had planted tomato and pepper plants there, hoping they'd be safe from the snails. Now, only a grey-green pepper stem remains. Sad, yet somehow looking splendid in the glistening mucus, splendid in its dying. I, too, want a color for myself, want to look splendid in death, not a mere dried husk, sapped. I want to leave a fiery trail in the darkness, a spent comet, colorful in dying defiance.

For now, I watch, wait, bide my time. It will come as certain as the snails do at night.

DUSTY

When I carry Dusty to her food
her spine knuckles through white fur
hindquarters sharp like bleached bones in the desert

When I call her she responds   blue eyes alert but
when the dog nuzzles her she does not swat or hiss
simply remains curled

> I feel tired today
> think of taking vitamins
> at least some iron

She does not dig into her food   does not drink
even when I dip my finger into the water to touch
her pursed mouth   I feel her ribcage through the fur

> I feel drawn as if something unknown
> was gnawing at me   draining me
> all I want is to curl up

At night I wake wonder if she's in pain   when I rise
I stumble over her body curled stiffly
into a spiney ball next to my bed

> Even though the sun is bright today
> my face looks waxen eyes puffed
> ribcage swollen

Sorry, there is nothing we can do for her...

> Food does not appeal to me
> I feel stifled stiff as if a furry blanket
> were wrapping itself around my ribs
>
> ...all I want is to curl up
> into a tiny ball at
> the foot of somebody's bed
> ...all I want is for someone
> to stroke my body...

DEMON MOUSE

It is dead
this little mouse which sent me
into a hysterical tailspin

I'd suspected it was here somewhere
scratching mysteriously at the corners
of my awareness   I denied its existence
because mice simply do not live in my house

Now its tiny carcass lies head severed
in my pantry   face peaceful
but I am afraid   shrinking from
the responsibility of removing it

I close the pantry door to wait for
my knight to come off the freeway
to valiantly dispose of
the death I created

Somehow the tiny death grows
gnaws beyond the closed door
I see enormous whiskers and darting
rodent eyes squeezing through the crack

Howling squeals of death send
enormous shivers up my spine
My own little demons claw at me but
I shut them down with a smile

DREAMSCAPE

I had no idea that she was there. Turning, casting her shadows on the walls of my room. As I busied myself, creating new sounds with old dishes, she moved silently and took something. I'm not sure what it was. Something real but invisible like friendship, like trust. Something you don't see, but tangible just the same. I knew, though I didn't actually see it, that she took something precious.

I felt the void, the assault, before I actually saw her. Standing, pale like a mere blue wisp of her former self, in my partially opened front door. She looked like a waifish, silent omen with the light behind her. Empty light. A barren landscape. A sense of empty canvas, a tremendously pale void surrounding her - a Dali painting. One bony hip thrust upward awkwardly yet sensuously providing a seat for a young child. She stood looking at me with parted silent lips, large limpid eyes - landscapes everywhere. Though I know it is she who stole from me, silently as it was behind the wall, I feel she is accusing me of something, imploring me.

Within the grey room, grey walls, cubes, squares, angles, the rectangular light splinters around the soft angles of the woman, refracting near her blonde hair, pale straw on fire, cheekbones and the caves of her eyes.

There is no sound. The only sound is that of the throbbing of my heart between my eyes.

WHO IS IT?

As I step into the dark garage, the sidedoor slams shut. It had been locked. Just before it closes completely, a sharp shadow grows toward me from the corner. Something is holding its breath. I stand mute, knowing that it will find me.

The telephone rings, loudly, somehow betraying my presence. The loud shrilling rolls down the hallway, out the backdoor to my feet, clamoring to be answered. My knees shake; my heart beats like a jungle drum. I take a small step and clang loudly and absurdly into the watering can which should not be standing there. Again, I see a fast Dervish of a shadow whirl past the garage window. Blindly, the Hounds of the Baskerville yapping at my heels, I run into the laundryroom, a rushing, gathering sound behind me. As I try to slam the door behind me, my skirt pocket snags on the knob. Wildly pulling and jerking, I rip the pocket free. Something thuds into the door. I push madly against it from the inside and turn the lock, bracing myself against the wood. My heart is a beating fist and sweat pours from my face. My breath strains against my teeth.

I feel more than hear it, that furtive scratching, tiny like the wings of a dying bird. Then, malevolent sounds penetrate the wood, so quickly, I'm not absolutely sure they were actually spoken.

"I'll get you yet..."

GETTING OLDER

A spreading stain
"this" has no connection with me

Blurring definitions
fading colors
bleeding blending
absorbed into other fabrics

I resist Damn Right I resist
tearing wider and wider
soon the rip can't be mended
connected any more

I am a pea pod open green
meant to be split
leaning over the sides
straining for breath

my step falters slides
snakes coil at my ankles
their tongues slither and hiss

CHECK-UP

The woman wore drab skirt and blouse
glasses thick like bottlebottoms
spoke with an English inflection
had a nice smile and mannerisms

It does help
if nurses and bureaucratic-type people
have a humanness about them
You need it when

Bedsteads grab you in iron embraces
bedpans nail you to the floor
flannel shirts expose your privateness
which is no longer private
since everyone has at least
looked into your innermost
pulsing red hot center
without giving anything in return

except warm antiseptic behaviour
dying chrysanthemums on the sill

and beyond
grey sparrows chirp about their freedom

UNENDING CYLES

moths
flutter
between thighs
smell of blood

in the rain
fluids pump
behind women's
folded hands

draining juices
absorbed by
arid ground
pungent

sticky
ready with
fruitless bearing

GAUGUIN REVISITED

pink sky touches purple to my garden
smears crimson onto six o'clock news
   dark green shadows spread
   beneath the chicken frying

from cool clay floor to sinking sunlight
arms stretch toward coconuts
evening clouds dance at the edge of shore
rinsing conch shells wading
drifting in the sand
sunwarm hair molding to my neck
flowered skirt lifting high above
my thighs and silver green water
tongues between my toes as I grow
become an immense woman
whose body loves the land
the sea caresses the sun molten
on the horizon huge child amid the stars
bronzed arms play among the gods
like Aphrodite in Zeus' lap
golden apples fall into the sea

spent I shrink
rinsing shells like any mortal
on the shore listening
to captive sounds gathered
buried deep inside
my womanhood soft
sandy ready to be molded

hot winds blow me back to
dark green and purple shadows
of my house.

SUMMERS PAST

sepia   tangy
the beach floats
on gulls' wings
ancient whisperings
meet waves and shore

hot sand scorches skin and
tender feet raw
pink sun paints glaring
rainbows behind shut eyes

yearnings deep within me
merge youth and
blistering dunes and
waves simmering
in glaring light

LATE DREAMING

the sun sits
bloodred in the evening sky
as I surface upward from
a numbing dispair
breast-stroking through traffic
rushing like draining water

all I want is to float
along the water's edge
listen to sucking waves
breathe deeply nighttime hues
greens lavenders trail my fingers
in rippling coolness
follow dizzying circles of waterbugs
tracing swirling silver shadows
of life beneath the surface

MAN-MADE

From peeling yellow window in Berkeley
bearded voice slithers
Nice tits! then tries to look
like a ventriloquist

black girl from stinking doorway
hisses *Got some change? Huh?*
then answers for me *Guess not today!*

from bright blue wall red paint screams
And Salvador will win! Fascist Pigs!
A house away beneath fire-gutted window
War is menstruation envy!

from the heat of a drugstore doorway
sun-bleached newspapers accuse grandmothers
and fathers of abusing children in their care

windows for exhibition, for shutting in, keeping out
doors for closing on subjects, opening new avenues
doors and windows, man-made frames without interiors
Man-made obstacles like commas
and periods to sentences

something to get through like the womb like guilt, quilt,
man-made guilt-quilt Think hard enough and frames,
boundaries and annihilation don't really exist
People don't really exist! Don't matter!
Annihilation a fascist pig! Kilroy and I were never here!

faceless voice flutters from bleached curtain
'F   OFF! DON'T HAVE TO ANSWER TO NOBODY!'

If this is true then I want to get off
this messed-up merry-go-round
But I'm angry and
want to leave red tracks
in the hot sand

A BERKELEY STREET CORNER

shivering Chihuahua against
cold ribs   Exposed in hunger
birds-of-a-feather
cold in these rags

>"gimme a dime   gimme love
>hey baby hey baby
>gimme...gimme.
>
>was young once
>yo black rock eyes
>hurt me no mo!
>
>rag brother
>got a joint?
>I ain't proud!"

same corner
same stink
same headlines

foreign nations
unravelling
famine pain famine pain

>"Looka hea!   Looka hea!
>Who's keepin' me company?
>
>Me and Chihuahua?   Yeah!
>Was rosy-cheeked once   Yeah!
>
>Now I write
>
>*No one lives hea*
>*No mo!*"

CAUGHT

I watch young people frown
into the ground splattered with light
green spring sun   grass pushing up
between the cracks   their shoes march
to whatever tune is
plugged into their ears

they do not see the new spring
songs in the wide blue sky
while I am here   caught
behind my windshield

bird who wants
to touch the wind

REFLECTION IN MIRROR

I don't want polyester years
ahead of me and pity in your eyes
remembering in others' ears of boredom
that I have been

I don't want to live until I forget
what life and us were all about
or might have been for you and me

I don't want to count days until the end
or wait to see where I've been
what's the point
unless you see (with me)
the silk in polyester

CHILLY SCENE

Winter came, softly

spreading icy bloom

upon fading light

blue fingers

fanned fading breath

soft bloom, silently

silver winter white

glowed softly

chilling breath

below

Fuer Vati

memories are flat
       stones unrounded
unwashed
by daylight's truth

I want to think
       imperfect stones   feel dents
bumps see discolorations
which were and are of us
and time rolled the stone

       rolled the stone
now I am like you
part of the landscape
and sun refracts off me
in the riverbed

I am burnished by your goodness
       your compassion   my thoughts
of past and present are round
smooth speckled stones

rolling
       curving
filling the spaces
as part of the whole

Onkel Walter

When I die
will you be brushing your teeth
hair or dog?

When you die
will I be writing or reading
some other dead person's soulful words
to sustain me throughout eternity?

The day my Uncle died he watered his grave
the family plot Went home to take the nap
from which he never awakened
Did he wonder what lay beneath the soil
that day? Did he think he was Prussian
or Bavarian when he dressed in the morning
Did he think about us?

I remember Uncle Walter's erect Prussian stance
and words I never quite understood because
his teeth never parted enough
His cold indifference as we children
passed him on the stairs And when we
left Germany he seemed glad to see us go
in truth   was part of the reason we left

I remember the old man he'd become when last I
saw him   Black hair now silver Proud cheekbones
turned pouches and wide shoulders dropped to
meet rising belly Still eyes blazed beneath bushy
brows as he sat on sagging sofa frustrated
by life itself His inability to harness it
like the horses he rode in the cavalry

Proud and Prussian   I remember him through
my child's eyes though I didn't really know the man
We were part of each other's history remote but true
My stranger uncle embarked on his silent journey
uniquely as he lived his life
Proud and Prussian

EULOGY

When a man dies, a whole world dies with him
the microscopic world which he created
for himself within this world

He lived the best way he knew how within
the confines of his world with his peculiar quirks
and characteristics which made him unique

It is for those unique qualities
that he will be remembered
for the new worlds which
he helped create and left behind
those of his children and grandchildren
his satellites within a boundless universe

In memory of A.J.F. Sr.

THE TOURIST

As we approach *Stadtpfarrkirche*, the church where I was baptized, I am anxious to round the corner, to roll back the time like a dusty carpet. A tourbus stops, expelling its load of colorful travellers.

My sister, my friends and I used to play ball games right in this spot, around the corner from my grandparents' house, and were accustomed to the busses and their curious crowd, the dazzle of strange languages and clothes. Eyes would flutter over us and at times we became permanent images in someone's camera. I used to wonder about the places these people had seen, where they lived, what they thought when they saw us children, our home. Now, I am a tourist of sorts myself and have brought my own family to travel through my childhood.

My heart quickens as I think about my grandparents' house. My sister, Christa, and I spent our summers here. Sultry, rainy summer days. Apple branches pulled deep in the garden, leaves round and metallic in the late afternoon light. Watching a torrential downpour leaning far out on the bedroom window sill. Whirlpools in the gutter, water gurgling and splashing out of the drainpipes, gushing downhill. I felt safe inside there, knowing the room behind me, loving the people across the hall. Eight and ten and twelve-year old safety which would last forever.

The room which my sister and I shared during those summers was usually cold. I remember the cold now because I know the American warmth. The room was narrow, high-ceilinged. Blue. A small desk underneath the deep windowsill. A narrow bed fitted into the far corner, high legs on a barren floor. A wooden wardrobe to the left of the door and in the desk drawer, an oboe. I blew into it often, imagining that I was eliciting pleasant sounds, seeing myself as a shepherdess on sun-drenched pastures.

The other window, to the right of the front door, belonged to the kitchen and then to my grandfather. In a manner of speaking, he held court there. The right half of the curtained window was usually opened inward. He stood just behind the sill in his dark twilled pants going through the ritual of pinching snuff, cleaning his meticulous moustache with a silver oval brush. Then, carefully, he brushed his bushy eyebrows. He leaned on the window sill and anyone on foot or on bike, stopped to chat with *Herr* Zinoni. Knowing how to spin a good yarn, he appreciated a good audience.

Christa and I were often behind him festooned on the kitchen sofa with its many embroidered pillows. We, too, wanted to be entertained by his colorful stories and intricate pencil drawings. We built castles with the pillows or read magazines which were delivered weekly by a man on a bicycle equipped with a large container. In it, in an orderly fashion, hung the much anticipated reading material which was then taken away by week's end and brought to other subscribers. We also listened to the large *Grundig* radio which was suspended kitty-corner above the sofa. Voices from exotic places like Belgravia and Budapest and Bing Crosby and Grace Kelly singing what sounded like a love-song sent delicious chills along my spine.

We have turned the corner. The house looks just like I thought it would. Wait - there are distortions. The white painted windows, the sturdy door, have been replaced with something modern, metallic. With an effort I restrain myself from knocking on the door, demanding to see the affronters of my carefully cultivated memories. My family watches me furtively from beneath lowered lashes feigning interest in the old neighborhood. Early evening shadows touch the windows. A cloud hangs in the reflection.

I stand rooted to the spot. As I look at the kitchen window now, this very ordinary window made more so by its vulgar modernity, I think of how much of a world was contained behind its glass.

Still reflected, I see the relatives who came to visit, often by train, who sat around the rectangular kitchen table. My sister and I helped to set the table with gold-rimmed cups and saucers, a glass bowl of fresh whipped cream, strong coffee, and my grandmother's *Zwetschgen Datschi* , the plum juice seeping into the yeast cake. The women talked or whispered from flowered or polka-dotted silk dresses made by the seamstress. The men bellowed from starched white collars, blue-shadowed and moustached faces. Corsets creaked. From large bosoms rose the fragrance of *Eau de Cologne* dabbed there. Pipe and cigar clouds hung thickly in the air. At the end of their visits, sometimes a new silver Mark piece found its way into our pink and empty palms. Quiet mice that we were, we had learned many a scandalous piece of gossip, recollections of the war or political opinions. This despite often being told, "Don't listen!" as if the order itself was enough to shut down the functions of our burning ears.

My son and daughter stray now into my visions of yester-day. Their present images lively overlays to my vivid mental ones. At their age, so close to my memory self, they've already seen and experienced so much more. In a way so much less. While I had had relatively little, my memories are brimming with simple sights and sounds but bold and lingering textures. At their age, I'd travelled two hours by train into my summers, yet they've crossed oceans and walked off the plane as though it were a train.

Mike scans the small alleyway next to the house, expecting the unexpected. He bends to coax a cat into view. Christy stands close to me, as she usually does, gauging her security. My husband, too, completing the triangle extend-ing from me, stands patiently. Silently, they linger, waiting for my next movement.

Suddenly, the front door opens. A strange lady comes out. Very modern, blonde, chic. Like the windows and doors, she does not fit into the picture. Her pale glance skips over me like flat stones skimming water. I feel compelled to speak to her. I say that my grandparents used to live here. It's only been two days since I've spoken German again, but to my dismay, I hear American sounding "things" creeping into my pronunciation. Her eyes slide over me as she   probably assumes that I left to marry an American and have now returned to put on airs. A common assumption, therefore a common cliche.

I feel like a beggar. I want something of which I am not sure. She hastens to say that she is also visiting. Says it as though she were ashamed of being connected with this place.

I glance at my family. Perhaps it is time to lay to sleep those restless memories and work on my own, enhancing the texture of the moment for my children.

The windows reflect an empty sky, the doorway is empty. There's nothing more to see.

LOOKING FOR DIRECTION IN BERLIN

"Prinz Regentenstrasse? You are American yes?"
I am offended by his yellow broken teeth
issuing bi-lingual   cultured information
on a cloud of rancid alcohol   I am offended
that he overlooked my German
which is still very good

His question holds me Spotlighted by the
streetlight's round glow and loud singing
to American jukebox music from the corner bar

"I vas prisoner of var   In Kalifornia" he shares
from gray-stubbled face   as if it mattered to me
or anyone   As we eye each other
across time and continents   Seconds stretch
I disown him his Germanness
as if it were my right
          My syllables hang mid-air

and so do memories   real and imagined
Unasked questions ripple far
History divides and unites us
          But it would be easier to ask
this stranger than my relatives
how they really feel about me and my

"American" family wholesome as
they are standing on the other side
waiting for me to disentangle myself
          with my perfect German
I cross the ill-lit street   The sidewalk recedes
my stride slows to a cakewalk on ice
          I have lost something

The stranger's eyes burn into my skull
pull me back to the other side
The echoes smolder

THE TUNNEL

Even though I am tired from the long flight and ride from Frankfurt to Donauwoerth, I take a stroll through the town. My mother's hometown, my birthplace. Afternoon sun slants into my path.

Ahead of me, an elderly woman, face of a dried apple doll, sweeps in front of her house with a twig broom. My grandmother used to chase us kids around the yard with her broom, intent on her target if she felt we had been disrespectful. Like my grandmother, this woman sees everything, knows that I am the American relative. I surprise her by greeting her in dialect. She responds in kind. Her eyes linger suspiciously on my jeans.

I pass Foerg's beauty salon. The first time I returned, I had my hair cut here. I had only been in the States five years, not enough time to change allegiance.

The second time I returned, I brought a husband. Seeing through his eyes allowed for a change of perspective, added other dimensions.

This time I've brought my entire family. My children, walking in the shadows of my childhood, are unaware that they somewhat replace the piece which had been removed with me.

On my bare arms, the light plays beige, white, yellow and warm. From the deepening afternoon shadows in the side streets comes the occasional clucking of a chicken, rises the smell of manure, flashes reflecting light from a kitchen window, opened to release cooking odors.

The traffic has thickened. Lumbering trucks, hauling timber, rattle their way down main street. The bright red rags hanging from their loads whip madly as they disappear toward the middle of town, across the square, toward the Danube Bridge, out onto the highway.

I must know every cobblestone on this road. There are new houses wedged in here and there; still I know this town like the lint in my pocket. I don't feel like a stranger, more like a native who's taken the long way around to get back.

Now I sit on an iron bench in the *Promenade*. My mother, her sisters and brother played here, patted the stone boy on the leaping dolphin by the fountain. The boy is still here, clinging to the mossy green rump of the petrified dolphin, stone hair flying like it did when I was a child.

From my childhood comes the taste of hot pretzels and lemon ice from Bundschuh's, the corner store. Out of the cool shadows from open doorways, the clean smell of wax, from the beer garden, the foamy malted smell from kegs, from the tobacconist's, the heady aroma of snuff and bundled tobacco leaves.

In that corner lot, a peacock strutted, spreading his shimmering brilliant fan, exoctic amid the brown, drab hens. Now, I see strange people there at long, wooden tables who are not playing *skat* like my grandfather and his card-playing friends did. These people look Iranian, speak something I don't understand. There is a kind of miniature golf terrain set up with grotesque plastic sunflowers twirling in the breeze.

From the sandbox in front of me spills grey sand the way it always has. There are imprints from this afternoon's youngsters but my own are there, too, deep inside. There, the big oak beyond the slight swell in the grass. We used to sprint from the oak to the sandbox, tumbling in as if it were a grey ocean.

To the left of the lawn, wide, graceful stone steps curve upward to the wrought iron gates of the school yard. I have a snapshot which shows my sister and me standing on the top step. We were heavily shadowed by linden trees. The sun tried to touch my sister's blonde hair, instead spilled heavy lattice work at our feet.

The criss-crossing shadows from bean and wysteria trellises are slanting into the white walkways now. Warm fingers of sun and cool purple shadows play around my feet.

My gaze follows the white pebbled walkways which converge on either side of the playground. Sweet, warm scents layer around me. Drifting from the river, the crimson smell of geraniums cascading over the city walls, the green dill smell from the gardens bordering the *Promenade*.

A bicycle bell disturbs my reverie. I rise and head toward the end of the park where an old tunnel leads to the banks of the Danube. We feared the tunnel, the unknown. I remember our children's voices, shrill with fear, our pounding feet, echoes rushing all around us. We had conquered every time we reached the end of the tunnel and the sun-washed smell of white stucco houses, the grove of pink-blooming apple trees, the sloping banks of the river.

I smile, enter the cool, dank cavity of the tunnel. The dampness is penetrating. Deep blue shadows and something dripping. I hear very faint laughter. Fear crawls to the back of my neck. Grown-ups don't run. I look toward the light. Vesper bells toll from Heilig Grab church. I hear the echoes.

THIN AIR.

It is my town again. Fleetingly, but mine.

Seven o'clock. The sky is streaked pink, grey and blue. Shadows are strong, outlining city hall in the river. The reflections quiver. For a shimmering moment, I see my own thirteen year-old smiling face.

Beneath the wooden planks, the water gushes over the locks. The water has kept me awake the last two nights. I look toward the other bridge spanning the river. So many bridges in this town, like a trick mirror. I used to ride my bicycle from one side of town to the other. Through the narrow cobblestone streets, beneath the railroad bridge, pumping through the arches of very old buildings, across parks and soccerfields, along the river, through the seasons.

Yesterday, I showed my old school to Mike and Christy. It has been twenty-seven years, but I know the curved stones through my thinly-soled shoes as though I'd never left. I want to imprint my yesterdays, a strong sense of place and continuity, a definite image within my children. Strangely, their being here seems to replace the pieces which were removed with me.

A young girl rounded the corner of the apothecary store. Her brown hair hung loosely to her shoulders, freckles spanned her nose and cheekbones. She pushed her bike, schoolbag slung above the rear tire. It was me.

There is no one nearby. Willows to my right hang heavily toward the water. It smells green like rivers seem to do. Violet shadows scurry beneath the water. There are secrets in the deepest parts of the willows. As the day rises, the panorama around me brightens and the bloodred petals of the geraniums on the bridge become more intense.

A close-up of time. On light green leaves, the dew drops shimmer blue and silvery. Water foams white, grey and powerfully beneath my feet. A window shutter bangs open sharply, a lacy curtain flutters outward and the smell of fresh, strong coffee. An old man walks his bike across the bridge, pants clipped together at the bottom. A shopping net hangs from his handlebars. His hands are gnarled. My grandfather's hands were ridged with the soil of the earth. I see strong hands fetching fresh, dripping sauerkraut out of the wooden barrel spooning it into my woolen mittens. I want to talk to the man as he walks into my memories but he has moved along trailing a stocky morning shadow.

I am an observer slotting my impressions like a postal clerk. Everything is clear to me, because my past is as real as the river beneath my feet. Still, I already feel the dull ache, once I've returned to the States, of wishing that I could stand here all over again. There is nothing new. The memories have simply met up with the moment.

Like an expected slight of hand, memory has merged with reality. My mind and my feelings dodge between remembered and present images. Reality is a mirage. You can't touch the past, you can't touch the present, in fact, it is already gone...it surrounds you like thin air.

EMIGRANT'S SONG

Come sit by me
toast and sing
to other times and places

Sway with me
remember why our
allegiance is divided

Feel with me
old sun and see
the gold of tomorrow

I need your yearnings
to meet with mine
in times of darkness

When you hear me speak
of other skies
and distant sorrows
when my heart bubbles
in ruby wine

Then, come once more
to sit with me
together we will braid
our songs into flowers
for tomorrow

About the Author:

Linda Foley captures us. In one tick of the clock, she opens our eyes and at the same time holds us in her embrace. "Come sit by me/ toast and sing..." she calls to us in "Emigrant's Song."

After immigrating to the United States at the age of 13 and settling in New York with her parents and sister, her first published article appeared in her hometown newspaper in southern Germany. She says "Language is free... a tool, a gift, accessible to everyone... it should be treated with utmost respect." With her flow of precise imagery, she connects past, present, and future in bold and lingering textures.

A poet and painter, Linda's prose pieces are every bit as good as her poems. She has an infallible sense of story. Her poetry and stories have appeared in: *Vintage '45, Maternal Legacy, Across The Generations, Poets Anonymous, Womankind*, and *Olympiad of Knowledge*, a medical journal. In 1985, she won The California Writers' Club award for fiction.

Esther Anderson

Photo by David M. Allen